50 Mexican-Inspired Recipes for Taco Night

By: Kelly Johnson

Table of Contents

- Classic Beef Tacos
- Chicken Tinga Tacos
- Fish Tacos with Cabbage Slaw
- Shrimp Tacos with Avocado Crema
- Vegetarian Black Bean Tacos
- Chorizo and Potato Tacos
- Barbacoa Tacos with Pickled Onions
- Pork Carnitas Tacos
- Mushroom and Spinach Tacos
- Sweet Potato and Black Bean Tacos
- Baja Fish Tacos with Spicy Mayo
- Tacos al Pastor with Pineapple Salsa
- Beef and Cheese Tacos with Salsa Verde
- Pulled Chicken Tacos with Cilantro Lime Rice
- Breakfast Tacos with Eggs and Chorizo
- Spicy Lentil Tacos
- BBQ Jackfruit Tacos
- Tacos de Pescado with Mango Salsa
- Stuffed Poblano Tacos
- Quinoa and Veggie Tacos
- Fire-Roasted Corn and Zucchini Tacos
- Chipotle Chicken Tacos with Avocado
- Ground Turkey Tacos with Cabbage Slaw
- Sesame Ginger Tofu Tacos
- Crispy Tacos with Beef and Cheese
- Coconut Shrimp Tacos with Sweet Chili Sauce
- Spicy Beef and Cheese Enchiladas
- Rajas Tacos with Grilled Peppers and Onions
- Classic Pork Tacos with Salsa Roja
- Buffalo Cauliflower Tacos with Blue Cheese Dressing

- Baked Taco Cups with Ground Beef
- Korean BBQ Tacos with Kimchi
- Fish Tacos with Cilantro Lime Dressing
- Spicy Chicken Tacos with Mango Salsa
- Sizzling Steak Tacos with Avocado Cream
- Lentil and Sweet Potato Tacos
- Tacos de Carnitas with Cilantro and Onion
- Roasted Vegetable Tacos with Feta
- Hawaiian BBQ Chicken Tacos
- Chipotle Black Bean Tacos with Corn Salsa
- Mahi Mahi Tacos with Cilantro Lime Sauce
- Turkey and Sweet Potato Tacos
- Tacos de Barbacoa with Red Chili Sauce
- Mexican Street Corn Tacos
- Vegetable Fajita Tacos
- Pork Belly Tacos with Jalapeño Slaw
- Crispy Chickpea Tacos
- Sriracha Shrimp Tacos with Avocado Salsa
- Taco Salad Bowls
- Mini Taco Cups with Taco Meat

Classic Beef Tacos

Ingredients:

- **For the Beef:**
    - 1 lb ground beef
    - 1 tablespoon vegetable oil
    - 1 small onion, finely chopped
    - 2 cloves garlic, minced
    - 1 tablespoon chili powder
    - 1 teaspoon cumin
    - 1 teaspoon paprika
    - ½ teaspoon salt
    - ¼ teaspoon black pepper
    - ½ cup beef broth or water
- **For the Tacos:**
    - 8 small corn or flour tortillas
    - 1 cup shredded lettuce
    - 1 cup diced tomatoes
    - 1 cup shredded cheese (cheddar or Mexican blend)
    - ½ cup sour cream
    - ¼ cup fresh cilantro, chopped
    - Lime wedges, for serving

Instructions:

1. **Cook the Beef:**
    - In a large skillet, heat the vegetable oil over medium heat. Add the chopped onion and sauté until translucent, about 3-4 minutes.
    - Stir in the minced garlic and cook for another minute until fragrant.
    - Add the ground beef, breaking it up with a spatula. Cook until browned and cooked through, about 5-7 minutes.
    - Drain excess fat if necessary, then stir in the chili powder, cumin, paprika, salt, and black pepper. Pour in the beef broth or water and simmer for 5 minutes until the mixture thickens slightly.
2. **Prepare the Tortillas:**
    - While the beef is cooking, warm the tortillas in a dry skillet over medium heat for about 30 seconds on each side or until soft and pliable. You can also wrap them in foil and warm them in the oven.

3. **Assemble the Tacos:**
    - Place a generous amount of the beef mixture in the center of each tortilla. Top with shredded lettuce, diced tomatoes, and shredded cheese.
    - Add a dollop of sour cream and sprinkle with fresh cilantro. Squeeze fresh lime juice over the top if desired.
4. **Serve:**
    - Serve the tacos immediately with lime wedges on the side for squeezing over the top.

Enjoy your classic beef tacos!

Feel free to adjust the toppings and spices to suit your taste!

Chicken Tinga Tacos

Ingredients:

- **For the Chicken Tinga:**
    - 1 lb boneless, skinless chicken thighs
    - 2 tablespoons vegetable oil
    - 1 small onion, finely chopped
    - 2 cloves garlic, minced
    - 1 can (14 oz) diced tomatoes
    - 2 chipotle peppers in adobo sauce, chopped
    - 1 teaspoon dried oregano
    - 1 teaspoon cumin
    - Salt and pepper to taste
- **For the Tacos:**
    - 8 small corn or flour tortillas
    - 1 cup crumbled queso fresco or feta cheese
    - 1 cup diced avocado
    - Fresh cilantro, for garnish
    - Lime wedges, for serving

Instructions:

1. **Prepare the Chicken Tinga:**
    - In a large skillet, heat vegetable oil over medium heat. Add the onion and garlic, cooking until softened, about 3-4 minutes.
    - Add the chicken thighs, diced tomatoes, chipotle peppers, oregano, and cumin. Season with salt and pepper.
    - Cover and simmer for 25-30 minutes, or until the chicken is cooked through. Remove the chicken and shred it with two forks, then return it to the skillet and stir to combine with the sauce.
2. **Warm the Tortillas:**
    - In a separate skillet, warm the tortillas over medium heat until soft and pliable.
3. **Assemble the Tacos:**
    - Fill each tortilla with the chicken tinga mixture. Top with crumbled cheese, diced avocado, and fresh cilantro. Serve with lime wedges on the side.

Fish Tacos with Cabbage Slaw

Ingredients:

- **For the Fish:**
    - 1 lb white fish fillets (such as cod or tilapia)
    - 1 teaspoon chili powder
    - 1 teaspoon cumin
    - Salt and pepper to taste
    - 2 tablespoons olive oil
    - 1 lime, juiced
- **For the Cabbage Slaw:**
    - 2 cups shredded green cabbage
    - 1 cup shredded red cabbage
    - 1 carrot, grated
    - ¼ cup mayonnaise
    - 1 tablespoon apple cider vinegar
    - 1 tablespoon lime juice
    - Salt and pepper to taste
- **For the Tacos:**
    - 8 small corn or flour tortillas
    - Fresh cilantro, for garnish
    - Lime wedges, for serving

Instructions:

1. **Prepare the Fish:**
    - In a bowl, mix together the chili powder, cumin, salt, and pepper. Rub this mixture over the fish fillets.
    - In a skillet, heat olive oil over medium-high heat. Add the fish and cook for about 4-5 minutes per side until cooked through and flaky. Squeeze lime juice over the fish before removing from heat.
2. **Make the Cabbage Slaw:**
    - In a large bowl, combine the shredded green and red cabbage and grated carrot. In a separate bowl, mix the mayonnaise, apple cider vinegar, lime juice, salt, and pepper. Pour the dressing over the cabbage mixture and toss to combine.
3. **Assemble the Tacos:**

- Warm the tortillas and fill each with a piece of fish and a generous spoonful of cabbage slaw. Garnish with fresh cilantro and serve with lime wedges.

Shrimp Tacos with Avocado Crema

Ingredients:

- **For the Shrimp:**
    - 1 lb large shrimp, peeled and deveined
    - 2 tablespoons olive oil
    - 1 teaspoon chili powder
    - 1 teaspoon cumin
    - ½ teaspoon garlic powder
    - Salt and pepper to taste
    - 1 lime, juiced
- **For the Avocado Crema:**
    - 1 ripe avocado
    - ½ cup sour cream or Greek yogurt
    - 1 lime, juiced
    - Salt to taste
- **For the Tacos:**
    - 8 small corn or flour tortillas
    - 1 cup shredded lettuce
    - 1 cup diced tomatoes
    - Fresh cilantro, for garnish
    - Lime wedges, for serving

Instructions:

1. **Prepare the Shrimp:**
    - In a bowl, combine shrimp with olive oil, chili powder, cumin, garlic powder, salt, and pepper. Toss to coat evenly.
    - In a skillet over medium-high heat, cook the shrimp for about 2-3 minutes per side until pink and cooked through. Squeeze lime juice over the shrimp before removing from heat.
2. **Make the Avocado Crema:**
    - In a blender or food processor, combine the avocado, sour cream, lime juice, and salt. Blend until smooth and creamy.
3. **Assemble the Tacos:**
    - Warm the tortillas and fill each with cooked shrimp. Top with shredded lettuce, diced tomatoes, and a drizzle of avocado crema. Garnish with fresh cilantro and serve with lime wedges.

Enjoy these flavorful taco recipes!

Vegetarian Black Bean Tacos

Ingredients:

- **For the Filling:**
    - 2 cans (15 oz each) black beans, rinsed and drained
    - 1 tablespoon olive oil
    - 1 small onion, finely chopped
    - 2 cloves garlic, minced
    - 1 teaspoon cumin
    - 1 teaspoon smoked paprika
    - Salt and pepper to taste
- **For the Tacos:**
    - 8 small corn or flour tortillas
    - 1 cup corn kernels (fresh or frozen)
    - 1 avocado, diced
    - 1 cup diced tomatoes
    - Fresh cilantro, for garnish
    - Lime wedges, for serving

Instructions:

1. **Prepare the Filling:**
    - In a skillet, heat olive oil over medium heat. Add the onion and garlic, cooking until softened, about 3-4 minutes.
    - Stir in the black beans, cumin, smoked paprika, salt, and pepper. Cook for another 5 minutes, mashing some of the beans for a creamier texture.
2. **Warm the Tortillas:**
    - Warm the tortillas in a dry skillet over medium heat until soft.
3. **Assemble the Tacos:**
    - Fill each tortilla with the black bean mixture, corn, diced avocado, and tomatoes. Garnish with fresh cilantro and serve with lime wedges.

Chorizo and Potato Tacos

Ingredients:

- **For the Filling:**
    - 1 lb chorizo sausage, casings removed
    - 2 medium potatoes, peeled and diced
    - 1 tablespoon vegetable oil
    - 1 small onion, chopped
    - 1 teaspoon cumin
    - Salt and pepper to taste
- **For the Tacos:**
    - 8 small corn or flour tortillas
    - 1 cup shredded lettuce
    - 1 cup diced tomatoes
    - Fresh cilantro, for garnish
    - Lime wedges, for serving

Instructions:

1. **Prepare the Filling:**
    - In a skillet, heat the vegetable oil over medium heat. Add the potatoes and cook until golden and tender, about 10-12 minutes. Remove and set aside.
    - In the same skillet, cook the chorizo over medium heat, breaking it apart until browned. Add the onions and cook until softened, about 3-4 minutes. Stir in the cooked potatoes, cumin, salt, and pepper.
2. **Warm the Tortillas:**
    - Warm the tortillas in a dry skillet over medium heat.
3. **Assemble the Tacos:**
    - Fill each tortilla with the chorizo and potato mixture. Top with shredded lettuce and diced tomatoes. Garnish with fresh cilantro and serve with lime wedges.

Barbacoa Tacos with Pickled Onions

Ingredients:

- **For the Barbacoa:**
    - 2 lbs beef chuck roast
    - 2 tablespoons vegetable oil
    - 1 onion, quartered
    - 4 cloves garlic, minced
    - 2 chipotle peppers in adobo sauce, chopped
    - 1 tablespoon cumin
    - 1 tablespoon oregano
    - 1 cup beef broth
    - Salt and pepper to taste
- **For the Pickled Onions:**
    - 1 red onion, thinly sliced
    - ½ cup vinegar (white or apple cider)
    - 1 tablespoon sugar
    - 1 teaspoon salt
- **For the Tacos:**
    - 8 small corn or flour tortillas
    - Fresh cilantro, for garnish
    - Lime wedges, for serving

Instructions:

1. **Prepare the Barbacoa:**
    - In a large skillet, heat vegetable oil over medium-high heat. Sear the beef on all sides until browned. Remove from heat.
    - In a slow cooker, combine the beef, onion, garlic, chipotle peppers, cumin, oregano, beef broth, salt, and pepper. Cook on low for 8 hours or until tender. Shred the beef with two forks.
2. **Make the Pickled Onions:**
    - In a bowl, combine vinegar, sugar, and salt. Add the sliced onion and let sit for at least 30 minutes.
3. **Warm the Tortillas:**
    - Warm the tortillas in a dry skillet over medium heat.
4. **Assemble the Tacos:**

- Fill each tortilla with barbacoa meat and top with pickled onions. Garnish with fresh cilantro and serve with lime wedges.

Pork Carnitas Tacos

Ingredients:

- **For the Carnitas:**
    - 3 lbs pork shoulder, cut into chunks
    - 1 onion, quartered
    - 4 cloves garlic, minced
    - 2 teaspoons cumin
    - 2 teaspoons oregano
    - 1 orange, juiced
    - 1 lime, juiced
    - Salt and pepper to taste
- **For the Tacos:**
    - 8 small corn or flour tortillas
    - 1 cup diced onions
    - 1 cup chopped cilantro
    - Lime wedges, for serving

Instructions:

1. **Prepare the Carnitas:**
    - In a slow cooker, combine the pork, onion, garlic, cumin, oregano, orange juice, lime juice, salt, and pepper. Cook on low for 8 hours or until tender. Shred the pork and broil for a few minutes for crispy edges.
2. **Warm the Tortillas:**
    - Warm the tortillas in a dry skillet over medium heat.
3. **Assemble the Tacos:**
    - Fill each tortilla with carnitas and top with diced onions and chopped cilantro. Serve with lime wedges.

Mushroom and Spinach Tacos

Ingredients:

- **For the Filling:**
    - 1 lb mushrooms, sliced
    - 2 cups fresh spinach
    - 2 tablespoons olive oil
    - 2 cloves garlic, minced
    - 1 teaspoon cumin
    - Salt and pepper to taste
- **For the Tacos:**
    - 8 small corn or flour tortillas
    - 1 cup crumbled feta cheese
    - Fresh cilantro, for garnish
    - Lime wedges, for serving

Instructions:

1. **Prepare the Filling:**
    - In a skillet, heat olive oil over medium heat. Add garlic and sauté for 1 minute. Add mushrooms and cook until browned, about 5-7 minutes. Stir in spinach, cumin, salt, and pepper until the spinach wilts.
2. **Warm the Tortillas:**
    - Warm the tortillas in a dry skillet over medium heat.
3. **Assemble the Tacos:**
    - Fill each tortilla with the mushroom and spinach mixture. Top with crumbled feta cheese and garnish with fresh cilantro. Serve with lime wedges.

Sweet Potato and Black Bean Tacos

Ingredients:

- **For the Filling:**
    - 2 medium sweet potatoes, peeled and diced
    - 1 can (15 oz) black beans, rinsed and drained
    - 2 tablespoons olive oil
    - 1 teaspoon chili powder
    - 1 teaspoon cumin
    - Salt and pepper to taste
- **For the Tacos:**
    - 8 small corn or flour tortillas
    - 1 avocado, diced
    - 1 cup diced tomatoes
    - Fresh cilantro, for garnish
    - Lime wedges, for serving

Instructions:

1. **Prepare the Filling:**
    - Preheat the oven to 400°F (200°C). Toss sweet potatoes with olive oil, chili powder, cumin, salt, and pepper. Spread on a baking sheet and roast for 25-30 minutes until tender.
    - In a bowl, combine roasted sweet potatoes and black beans.
2. **Warm the Tortillas:**
    - Warm the tortillas in a dry skillet over medium heat.
3. **Assemble the Tacos:**
    - Fill each tortilla with the sweet potato and black bean mixture. Top with diced avocado and tomatoes. Garnish with fresh cilantro and serve with lime wedges.

Baja Fish Tacos with Spicy Mayo

Ingredients:

- **For the Fish:**
    - 1 lb white fish fillets (such as cod or tilapia)
    - 1 cup all-purpose flour
    - 1 teaspoon chili powder
    - 1 teaspoon cumin
    - Salt and pepper to taste
    - 1 cup beer or sparkling water (for batter)
    - Vegetable oil for frying
- **For the Spicy Mayo:**
    - ½ cup mayonnaise
    - 1 tablespoon Sriracha or to taste
    - 1 teaspoon lime juice
- **For the Tacos:**
    - 8 small corn tortillas
    - 2 cups shredded cabbage
    - Fresh cilantro, for garnish
    - Lime wedges, for serving

Instructions:

1. **Prepare the Fish:**
    - In a bowl, combine flour, chili powder, cumin, salt, and pepper. Gradually whisk in beer or sparkling water until smooth.
    - Heat vegetable oil in a deep skillet over medium-high heat. Dip fish fillets into the batter and fry until golden and cooked through, about 3-4 minutes per side. Drain on paper towels.
2. **Make the Spicy Mayo:**
    - In a small bowl, mix mayonnaise, Sriracha, and lime juice until well combined.
3. **Warm the Tortillas:**
    - Warm the tortillas in a dry skillet over medium heat.
4. **Assemble the Tacos:**
    - Fill each tortilla with fried fish, top with shredded cabbage, and drizzle with spicy mayo. Garnish with fresh cilantro and serve with lime wedges.

Feel free to adjust the recipes and toppings to suit your taste!

Tacos al Pastor with Pineapple Salsa

Ingredients:

- **For the Al Pastor:**
    - 2 lbs pork shoulder, thinly sliced
    - 1/2 cup pineapple juice
    - 1/4 cup white vinegar
    - 2 cloves garlic, minced
    - 2 tablespoons adobo sauce
    - 1 tablespoon chili powder
    - 1 teaspoon cumin
    - 1 teaspoon oregano
    - Salt and pepper to taste
    - 1 cup diced pineapple (for salsa)
- **For the Pineapple Salsa:**
    - 1 cup diced pineapple
    - 1/2 red onion, finely chopped
    - 1 jalapeño, minced
    - Juice of 1 lime
    - Salt and pepper to taste
- **For the Tacos:**
    - 8 small corn or flour tortillas
    - Fresh cilantro, for garnish
    - Lime wedges, for serving

Instructions:

1. **Prepare the Al Pastor:**
    - In a bowl, combine pork, pineapple juice, vinegar, garlic, adobo sauce, chili powder, cumin, oregano, salt, and pepper. Marinate for at least 1 hour, preferably overnight.
    - Cook marinated pork in a skillet over medium heat until cooked through and slightly caramelized, about 10-15 minutes.
2. **Make the Pineapple Salsa:**
    - In a bowl, combine diced pineapple, red onion, jalapeño, lime juice, salt, and pepper. Set aside.
3. **Warm the Tortillas:**
    - Warm the tortillas in a dry skillet over medium heat.

4. **Assemble the Tacos:**
    - Fill each tortilla with al pastor pork and top with pineapple salsa. Garnish with fresh cilantro and serve with lime wedges.

Beef and Cheese Tacos with Salsa Verde

Ingredients:

- **For the Filling:**
    - 1 lb ground beef
    - 1 tablespoon olive oil
    - 1 small onion, chopped
    - 2 cloves garlic, minced
    - 1 teaspoon cumin
    - Salt and pepper to taste
    - 1 cup shredded cheese (cheddar or Mexican blend)
- **For the Salsa Verde:**
    - 1 cup tomatillos, husked and chopped
    - 1/2 onion, chopped
    - 1 jalapeño, chopped
    - 1/4 cup cilantro
    - Juice of 1 lime
    - Salt to taste
- **For the Tacos:**
    - 8 small corn or flour tortillas
    - Fresh cilantro, for garnish
    - Lime wedges, for serving

Instructions:

1. **Prepare the Beef Filling:**
    - In a skillet, heat olive oil over medium heat. Add onion and garlic, cooking until softened.
    - Add ground beef, cumin, salt, and pepper. Cook until browned and cooked through. Stir in shredded cheese until melted.
2. **Make the Salsa Verde:**
    - In a blender, combine tomatillos, onion, jalapeño, cilantro, lime juice, and salt. Blend until smooth.
3. **Warm the Tortillas:**
    - Warm the tortillas in a dry skillet over medium heat.
4. **Assemble the Tacos:**
    - Fill each tortilla with the beef mixture and drizzle with salsa verde. Garnish with fresh cilantro and serve with lime wedges.

Pulled Chicken Tacos with Cilantro Lime Rice

Ingredients:

- **For the Pulled Chicken:**
    - 2 lbs boneless, skinless chicken breasts
    - 1 cup chicken broth
    - 1 tablespoon taco seasoning
    - Salt and pepper to taste
- **For the Cilantro Lime Rice:**
    - 1 cup long-grain rice
    - 2 cups water
    - Juice of 1 lime
    - 1/4 cup chopped cilantro
    - Salt to taste
- **For the Tacos:**
    - 8 small corn or flour tortillas
    - 1 cup diced tomatoes
    - 1 avocado, sliced
    - Fresh cilantro, for garnish
    - Lime wedges, for serving

Instructions:

1. **Prepare the Pulled Chicken:**
    - In a slow cooker, combine chicken, chicken broth, taco seasoning, salt, and pepper. Cook on low for 6-8 hours until tender. Shred the chicken with two forks.
2. **Make the Cilantro Lime Rice:**
    - In a pot, combine rice and water. Bring to a boil, then reduce heat, cover, and simmer for 15-20 minutes until cooked. Stir in lime juice, cilantro, and salt.
3. **Warm the Tortillas:**
    - Warm the tortillas in a dry skillet over medium heat.
4. **Assemble the Tacos:**
    - Fill each tortilla with pulled chicken and cilantro lime rice. Top with diced tomatoes and avocado. Garnish with fresh cilantro and serve with lime wedges.

Breakfast Tacos with Eggs and Chorizo

Ingredients:

- **For the Filling:**
    - 1 lb chorizo sausage, casings removed
    - 6 large eggs
    - 1/4 cup milk
    - Salt and pepper to taste
- **For the Tacos:**
    - 8 small corn or flour tortillas
    - 1 cup shredded cheese (cheddar or Mexican blend)
    - 1 avocado, diced
    - Fresh cilantro, for garnish
    - Salsa, for serving

Instructions:

1. **Prepare the Filling:**
    - In a skillet, cook chorizo over medium heat until browned. In a bowl, whisk together eggs, milk, salt, and pepper. Pour into the skillet with chorizo and scramble until eggs are set.
2. **Warm the Tortillas:**
    - Warm the tortillas in a dry skillet over medium heat.
3. **Assemble the Tacos:**
    - Fill each tortilla with the chorizo and egg mixture. Top with shredded cheese, diced avocado, and garnish with fresh cilantro. Serve with salsa.

Spicy Lentil Tacos

Ingredients:

- **For the Filling:**
    - 1 cup lentils, rinsed
    - 2 cups vegetable broth
    - 1 small onion, chopped
    - 2 cloves garlic, minced
    - 1 teaspoon chili powder
    - 1 teaspoon cumin
    - 1/2 teaspoon cayenne pepper (adjust to taste)
    - Salt and pepper to taste
- **For the Tacos:**
    - 8 small corn or flour tortillas
    - 1 cup diced tomatoes
    - 1 avocado, diced
    - Fresh cilantro, for garnish
    - Lime wedges, for serving

Instructions:

1. **Prepare the Filling:**
    - In a pot, combine lentils and vegetable broth. Bring to a boil, then reduce heat and simmer for 20-25 minutes until tender.
    - In a skillet, sauté onion and garlic until softened. Stir in cooked lentils, chili powder, cumin, cayenne pepper, salt, and pepper. Cook for another 5 minutes.
2. **Warm the Tortillas:**
    - Warm the tortillas in a dry skillet over medium heat.
3. **Assemble the Tacos:**
    - Fill each tortilla with the lentil mixture. Top with diced tomatoes and avocado. Garnish with fresh cilantro and serve with lime wedges.

BBQ Jackfruit Tacos

Ingredients:

- **For the Filling:**
    - 2 cans (20 oz each) young green jackfruit in water, drained and shredded
    - 1 cup BBQ sauce
    - 1 tablespoon olive oil
    - 1 small onion, chopped
    - 2 cloves garlic, minced
    - Salt and pepper to taste
- **For the Tacos:**
    - 8 small corn or flour tortillas
    - 1 cup coleslaw (optional)
    - Fresh cilantro, for garnish
    - Lime wedges, for serving

Instructions:

1. **Prepare the Jackfruit Filling:**
    - In a skillet, heat olive oil over medium heat. Sauté onion and garlic until softened. Add shredded jackfruit and BBQ sauce, cooking for 10-15 minutes until heated through. Season with salt and pepper.
2. **Warm the Tortillas:**
    - Warm the tortillas in a dry skillet over medium heat.
3. **Assemble the Tacos:**
    - Fill each tortilla with BBQ jackfruit. Top with coleslaw if desired. Garnish with fresh cilantro and serve with lime wedges.

Tacos de Pescado with Mango Salsa

Ingredients:

- **For the Fish:**
    - 1 lb white fish fillets (such as tilapia or cod)
    - 1 cup all-purpose flour
    - 1 teaspoon chili powder
    - 1 teaspoon cumin
    - Salt and pepper to taste
    - Vegetable oil for frying
- **For the Mango Salsa:**
    - 1 ripe mango, diced
    - 1/2 red onion, finely chopped
    - 1 jalapeño, minced
    - Juice of 1 lime
    - Salt to taste
- **For the Tacos:**
    - 8 small corn tortillas
    - 2 cups shredded cabbage
    - Fresh cilantro, for garnish
    - Lime wedges, for serving

Instructions:

1. **Prepare the Fish:**
    - In a bowl, combine flour, chili powder, cumin, salt, and pepper. Dredge fish fillets in the flour mixture.
    - In a skillet, heat vegetable oil over medium-high heat. Fry fish for 3-4 minutes per side until golden and cooked through. Drain on paper towels.
2. **Make the Mango Salsa:**
    - In a bowl, combine diced mango, red onion, jalapeño, lime juice, and salt. Set aside.
3. **Warm the Tortillas:**
    - Warm the tortillas in a dry skillet over medium heat.
4. **Assemble the Tacos:**
    - Fill each tortilla with fried fish, top with shredded cabbage, and drizzle with mango salsa. Garnish with fresh cilantro and serve with lime wedges.

Feel free to adjust the recipes and toppings to suit your taste!

Stuffed Poblano Tacos

Ingredients:

- **For the Stuffed Poblano:**
    - 4 large poblano peppers
    - 1 cup cooked rice (white or brown)
    - 1 can (15 oz) black beans, rinsed and drained
    - 1 cup corn (fresh or frozen)
    - 1 teaspoon cumin
    - 1 teaspoon chili powder
    - Salt and pepper to taste
    - 1 cup shredded cheese (cheddar or Mexican blend)
- **For the Tacos:**
    - 8 small corn or flour tortillas
    - Fresh cilantro, for garnish
    - Lime wedges, for serving

Instructions:

1. **Prepare the Stuffed Poblano:**
    - Preheat the oven to 375°F (190°C). Cut the tops off the poblano peppers and remove the seeds.
    - In a bowl, mix cooked rice, black beans, corn, cumin, chili powder, salt, and pepper. Stuff the mixture into the poblano peppers and place them in a baking dish. Sprinkle cheese on top and bake for 25-30 minutes until the peppers are tender and the cheese is melted.
2. **Warm the Tortillas:**
    - Warm the tortillas in a dry skillet over medium heat.
3. **Assemble the Tacos:**
    - Slice the stuffed poblano peppers and fill each tortilla with the mixture. Garnish with fresh cilantro and serve with lime wedges.

Quinoa and Veggie Tacos

Ingredients:

- **For the Filling:**
    - 1 cup quinoa, rinsed
    - 2 cups vegetable broth
    - 1 tablespoon olive oil
    - 1 small onion, chopped
    - 1 bell pepper, chopped
    - 1 zucchini, diced
    - 1 teaspoon cumin
    - Salt and pepper to taste
- **For the Tacos:**
    - 8 small corn or flour tortillas
    - 1 avocado, sliced
    - Fresh cilantro, for garnish
    - Lime wedges, for serving

Instructions:

1. **Prepare the Quinoa and Veggie Filling:**
    - In a pot, combine quinoa and vegetable broth. Bring to a boil, then reduce heat and simmer for 15-20 minutes until quinoa is cooked and fluffy.
    - In a skillet, heat olive oil over medium heat. Sauté onion, bell pepper, and zucchini until tender. Stir in cooked quinoa, cumin, salt, and pepper.
2. **Warm the Tortillas:**
    - Warm the tortillas in a dry skillet over medium heat.
3. **Assemble the Tacos:**
    - Fill each tortilla with the quinoa and veggie mixture. Top with sliced avocado and garnish with fresh cilantro. Serve with lime wedges.

Fire-Roasted Corn and Zucchini Tacos

Ingredients:

- **For the Filling:**
    - 2 cups corn (fresh or frozen)
    - 2 medium zucchinis, diced
    - 1 tablespoon olive oil
    - 1 teaspoon smoked paprika
    - Salt and pepper to taste
- **For the Tacos:**
    - 8 small corn or flour tortillas
    - 1 cup crumbled feta cheese (optional)
    - Fresh cilantro, for garnish
    - Lime wedges, for serving

Instructions:

1. **Prepare the Filling:**
    - In a skillet, heat olive oil over medium heat. Add corn and zucchini, cooking until tender and slightly charred. Stir in smoked paprika, salt, and pepper.
2. **Warm the Tortillas:**
    - Warm the tortillas in a dry skillet over medium heat.
3. **Assemble the Tacos:**
    - Fill each tortilla with the corn and zucchini mixture. Top with crumbled feta cheese if desired. Garnish with fresh cilantro and serve with lime wedges.

Chipotle Chicken Tacos with Avocado

Ingredients:

- **For the Chicken:**
    - 1 lb boneless, skinless chicken breasts
    - 2 tablespoons chipotle sauce (canned or homemade)
    - Salt and pepper to taste
- **For the Tacos:**
    - 8 small corn or flour tortillas
    - 1 avocado, sliced
    - 1/2 cup diced red onion
    - Fresh cilantro, for garnish
    - Lime wedges, for serving

Instructions:

1. **Prepare the Chicken:**
    - In a bowl, mix chipotle sauce with salt and pepper. Coat chicken breasts with the mixture.
    - Cook chicken in a skillet over medium heat for about 6-7 minutes per side or until cooked through. Slice into strips.
2. **Warm the Tortillas:**
    - Warm the tortillas in a dry skillet over medium heat.
3. **Assemble the Tacos:**
    - Fill each tortilla with sliced chicken, top with avocado, and diced red onion. Garnish with fresh cilantro and serve with lime wedges.

Ground Turkey Tacos with Cabbage Slaw

Ingredients:

- **For the Turkey Filling:**
    - 1 lb ground turkey
    - 1 tablespoon olive oil
    - 1 small onion, chopped
    - 2 cloves garlic, minced
    - 1 teaspoon cumin
    - 1 teaspoon chili powder
    - Salt and pepper to taste
- **For the Cabbage Slaw:**
    - 2 cups shredded cabbage (green or purple)
    - 1/2 cup carrots, shredded
    - 1/4 cup mayonnaise
    - Juice of 1 lime
    - Salt and pepper to taste
- **For the Tacos:**
    - 8 small corn or flour tortillas
    - Fresh cilantro, for garnish
    - Lime wedges, for serving

Instructions:

1. **Prepare the Turkey Filling:**
    - In a skillet, heat olive oil over medium heat. Sauté onion and garlic until softened. Add ground turkey, cumin, chili powder, salt, and pepper. Cook until turkey is browned and cooked through.
2. **Make the Cabbage Slaw:**
    - In a bowl, combine shredded cabbage, carrots, mayonnaise, lime juice, salt, and pepper. Mix well.
3. **Warm the Tortillas:**
    - Warm the tortillas in a dry skillet over medium heat.
4. **Assemble the Tacos:**
    - Fill each tortilla with turkey filling and top with cabbage slaw. Garnish with fresh cilantro and serve with lime wedges.

Sesame Ginger Tofu Tacos

Ingredients:

- **For the Tofu:**
    - 1 block (14 oz) firm tofu, pressed and cubed
    - 2 tablespoons soy sauce
    - 1 tablespoon sesame oil
    - 1 tablespoon ginger, grated
    - 1 tablespoon garlic, minced
- **For the Tacos:**
    - 8 small corn or flour tortillas
    - 1 cup shredded carrots
    - 1 cup sliced cucumber
    - 1/4 cup chopped green onions
    - Fresh cilantro, for garnish
    - Lime wedges, for serving

Instructions:

1. **Prepare the Tofu:**
    - In a bowl, combine soy sauce, sesame oil, ginger, and garlic. Toss tofu cubes in the marinade and let sit for at least 30 minutes.
    - In a skillet, cook marinated tofu over medium heat until golden and crispy.
2. **Warm the Tortillas:**
    - Warm the tortillas in a dry skillet over medium heat.
3. **Assemble the Tacos:**
    - Fill each tortilla with crispy tofu and top with shredded carrots, sliced cucumber, and green onions. Garnish with fresh cilantro and serve with lime wedges.

Crispy Tacos with Beef and Cheese

Ingredients:

- **For the Beef Filling:**
    - 1 lb ground beef
    - 1 tablespoon olive oil
    - 1 small onion, chopped
    - 2 cloves garlic, minced
    - 1 teaspoon chili powder
    - 1 teaspoon cumin
    - Salt and pepper to taste
    - 1 cup shredded cheese (cheddar or Mexican blend)
- **For the Tacos:**
    - 8 taco shells (hard or soft)
    - Shredded lettuce, for garnish
    - Diced tomatoes, for garnish
    - Sour cream, for serving
    - Salsa, for serving

Instructions:

1. **Prepare the Beef Filling:**
    - In a skillet, heat olive oil over medium heat. Sauté onion and garlic until softened. Add ground beef, chili powder, cumin, salt, and pepper. Cook until browned and cooked through. Stir in shredded cheese until melted.
2. **Crisp the Taco Shells:**
    - If using soft tortillas, crisp them in the oven or on a skillet until golden and crunchy.
3. **Assemble the Tacos:**
    - Fill each taco shell with the beef mixture. Top with shredded lettuce and diced tomatoes. Serve with sour cream and salsa on the side.

Feel free to customize these recipes with your favorite toppings and ingredients!

Coconut Shrimp Tacos with Sweet Chili Sauce

Ingredients:

- **For the Coconut Shrimp:**
    - 1 lb large shrimp, peeled and deveined
    - 1/2 cup all-purpose flour
    - 2 large eggs, beaten
    - 1 cup shredded coconut
    - Salt and pepper to taste
    - Vegetable oil, for frying
- **For the Tacos:**
    - 8 small corn or flour tortillas
    - 1 cup shredded cabbage
    - 1/2 cup sweet chili sauce
    - Fresh cilantro, for garnish
    - Lime wedges, for serving

Instructions:

1. **Prepare the Coconut Shrimp:**
    - Season the shrimp with salt and pepper. Dredge each shrimp in flour, dip in beaten eggs, and then coat with shredded coconut.
    - In a skillet, heat vegetable oil over medium-high heat. Fry shrimp for 2-3 minutes per side until golden and cooked through. Drain on paper towels.
2. **Warm the Tortillas:**
    - Warm the tortillas in a dry skillet over medium heat.
3. **Assemble the Tacos:**
    - Fill each tortilla with shredded cabbage and fried coconut shrimp. Drizzle with sweet chili sauce and garnish with fresh cilantro. Serve with lime wedges.

Spicy Beef and Cheese Enchiladas

Ingredients:

- **For the Filling:**
    - 1 lb ground beef
    - 1 small onion, chopped
    - 2 cloves garlic, minced
    - 1 teaspoon chili powder
    - 1 teaspoon cumin
    - Salt and pepper to taste
    - 1 cup shredded cheese (cheddar or Mexican blend)
- **For the Enchiladas:**
    - 8 corn tortillas
    - 2 cups red enchilada sauce
    - 1 cup shredded cheese (cheddar or Mexican blend)
    - Fresh cilantro, for garnish
    - Sour cream, for serving

Instructions:

1. **Prepare the Beef Filling:**
    - In a skillet, sauté onion and garlic until softened. Add ground beef, chili powder, cumin, salt, and pepper. Cook until browned. Stir in 1 cup of cheese.
2. **Assemble the Enchiladas:**
    - Preheat the oven to 350°F (175°C). Soften tortillas in a hot skillet. Fill each tortilla with beef mixture and roll tightly.
    - Place enchiladas in a baking dish, cover with enchilada sauce, and sprinkle with remaining cheese. Bake for 20 minutes until cheese is melted and bubbly.
3. **Serve:**
    - Garnish with fresh cilantro and serve with sour cream.

Rajas Tacos with Grilled Peppers and Onions

Ingredients:

- **For the Filling:**
    - 2 large poblano peppers, roasted and sliced
    - 1 large onion, sliced
    - 2 tablespoons olive oil
    - Salt and pepper to taste
    - 1 cup crumbled queso fresco
- **For the Tacos:**
    - 8 small corn or flour tortillas
    - Fresh cilantro, for garnish
    - Lime wedges, for serving

Instructions:

1. **Prepare the Rajas:**
    - In a skillet, heat olive oil over medium heat. Sauté sliced onion until translucent. Add roasted poblano peppers and cook until heated through. Season with salt and pepper.
2. **Warm the Tortillas:**
    - Warm the tortillas in a dry skillet over medium heat.
3. **Assemble the Tacos:**
    - Fill each tortilla with rajas and top with crumbled queso fresco. Garnish with fresh cilantro and serve with lime wedges.

Classic Pork Tacos with Salsa Roja

Ingredients:

- **For the Pork Filling:**
    - 1 lb pork shoulder, cooked and shredded
    - 1 tablespoon olive oil
    - 1 teaspoon cumin
    - Salt and pepper to taste
- **For the Salsa Roja:**
    - 4 medium tomatoes, roasted
    - 1 small onion, chopped
    - 2 cloves garlic
    - 1-2 jalapeños, roasted
    - Salt to taste
- **For the Tacos:**
    - 8 small corn or flour tortillas
    - Fresh cilantro, for garnish
    - Lime wedges, for serving

Instructions:

1. **Prepare the Salsa Roja:**
    - Blend roasted tomatoes, onion, garlic, jalapeños, and salt until smooth. Set aside.
2. **Prepare the Pork Filling:**
    - In a skillet, heat olive oil over medium heat. Add shredded pork, cumin, salt, and pepper. Cook until heated through.
3. **Warm the Tortillas:**
    - Warm the tortillas in a dry skillet over medium heat.
4. **Assemble the Tacos:**
    - Fill each tortilla with the pork filling, drizzle with salsa roja, and garnish with fresh cilantro. Serve with lime wedges.

Buffalo Cauliflower Tacos with Blue Cheese Dressing

Ingredients:

- **For the Buffalo Cauliflower:**
    - 1 head of cauliflower, cut into florets
    - 1/2 cup buffalo sauce
    - 1 tablespoon olive oil
    - Salt and pepper to taste
- **For the Tacos:**
    - 8 small corn or flour tortillas
    - 1/2 cup crumbled blue cheese
    - 1 cup shredded lettuce
    - 1/2 cup ranch or blue cheese dressing
    - Fresh cilantro, for garnish

Instructions:

1. **Prepare the Buffalo Cauliflower:**
    - Preheat the oven to 425°F (220°C). Toss cauliflower florets with olive oil, salt, pepper, and buffalo sauce. Spread on a baking sheet and roast for 25-30 minutes until crispy.
2. **Warm the Tortillas:**
    - Warm the tortillas in a dry skillet over medium heat.
3. **Assemble the Tacos:**
    - Fill each tortilla with roasted buffalo cauliflower, top with shredded lettuce, crumbled blue cheese, and drizzle with dressing. Garnish with fresh cilantro.

Baked Taco Cups with Ground Beef

Ingredients:

- **For the Filling:**
    - 1 lb ground beef
    - 1 small onion, chopped
    - 1 tablespoon taco seasoning
    - Salt and pepper to taste
- **For the Taco Cups:**
    - 1 package of wonton wrappers
    - 1 cup shredded cheese (cheddar or Mexican blend)
    - 1 cup diced tomatoes
    - Sour cream, for serving
    - Fresh cilantro, for garnish

Instructions:

1. **Prepare the Beef Filling:**
    - In a skillet, sauté onion until softened. Add ground beef, taco seasoning, salt, and pepper. Cook until browned.
2. **Assemble the Taco Cups:**
    - Preheat the oven to 350°F (175°C). Lightly grease a muffin tin. Press wonton wrappers into the muffin cups, forming a cup shape. Fill each cup with beef filling and top with shredded cheese.
    - Bake for 15-20 minutes until wrappers are crispy and cheese is melted.
3. **Serve:**
    - Top with diced tomatoes, sour cream, and fresh cilantro before serving.

Korean BBQ Tacos with Kimchi

Ingredients:

- **For the Beef:**
    - 1 lb flank steak or beef short ribs
    - 1/4 cup soy sauce
    - 2 tablespoons brown sugar
    - 1 tablespoon sesame oil
    - 1 tablespoon garlic, minced
    - 1 tablespoon ginger, minced
- **For the Tacos:**
    - 8 small corn or flour tortillas
    - 1 cup kimchi
    - 1/4 cup chopped green onions
    - Fresh cilantro, for garnish
    - Lime wedges, for serving

Instructions:

1. **Prepare the Beef:**
    - In a bowl, combine soy sauce, brown sugar, sesame oil, garlic, and ginger. Marinate the beef in the mixture for at least 30 minutes or overnight.
    - Grill or pan-sear the marinated beef until cooked to your desired doneness. Let rest before slicing.
2. **Warm the Tortillas:**
    - Warm the tortillas in a dry skillet over medium heat.
3. **Assemble the Tacos:**
    - Fill each tortilla with sliced beef, top with kimchi, and sprinkle with chopped green onions. Garnish with fresh cilantro and serve with lime wedges.

Feel free to mix and match toppings and ingredients to suit your taste!

Fish Tacos with Cilantro Lime Dressing

Ingredients:

- **For the Fish:**
    - 1 lb white fish fillets (like cod or tilapia)
    - 2 tablespoons olive oil
    - 1 teaspoon chili powder
    - 1 teaspoon cumin
    - Salt and pepper to taste
    - 8 small corn or flour tortillas
- **For the Cilantro Lime Dressing:**
    - 1/2 cup Greek yogurt or sour cream
    - 1/4 cup fresh cilantro, chopped
    - Juice of 1 lime
    - Salt to taste
- **Toppings:**
    - Shredded cabbage
    - Diced tomatoes
    - Sliced avocado
    - Lime wedges

Instructions:

1. **Prepare the Fish:**
    - Preheat the grill or a skillet over medium-high heat. In a bowl, mix olive oil, chili powder, cumin, salt, and pepper. Coat the fish with the mixture.
    - Grill or cook the fish for 3-4 minutes per side until cooked through. Flake the fish into pieces.
2. **Make the Dressing:**
    - In a small bowl, combine Greek yogurt, cilantro, lime juice, and salt. Mix well.
3. **Warm the Tortillas:**
    - Warm the tortillas in a dry skillet over medium heat.
4. **Assemble the Tacos:**
    - Fill each tortilla with fish, drizzle with cilantro lime dressing, and top with shredded cabbage, diced tomatoes, and sliced avocado. Serve with lime wedges.

Spicy Chicken Tacos with Mango Salsa

Ingredients:

- **For the Chicken:**
    - 1 lb chicken breasts, diced
    - 2 tablespoons olive oil
    - 1 tablespoon taco seasoning
    - Salt and pepper to taste
    - 8 small corn or flour tortillas
- **For the Mango Salsa:**
    - 1 ripe mango, diced
    - 1/2 red onion, finely chopped
    - 1 jalapeño, minced
    - Juice of 1 lime
    - Salt to taste
    - Fresh cilantro, for garnish

Instructions:

1. **Prepare the Chicken:**
    - In a skillet, heat olive oil over medium heat. Add diced chicken, taco seasoning, salt, and pepper. Cook until chicken is cooked through and browned.
2. **Make the Mango Salsa:**
    - In a bowl, combine diced mango, red onion, jalapeño, lime juice, and salt. Mix well and garnish with fresh cilantro.
3. **Warm the Tortillas:**
    - Warm the tortillas in a dry skillet over medium heat.
4. **Assemble the Tacos:**
    - Fill each tortilla with spicy chicken and top with mango salsa. Serve immediately.

Sizzling Steak Tacos with Avocado Cream

Ingredients:

- **For the Steak:**
    - 1 lb flank steak, sliced thin
    - 2 tablespoons olive oil
    - 2 teaspoons taco seasoning
    - Salt and pepper to taste
    - 8 small corn or flour tortillas
- **For the Avocado Cream:**
    - 1 ripe avocado
    - 1/4 cup sour cream or Greek yogurt
    - Juice of 1 lime
    - Salt to taste
- **Toppings:**
    - Sliced radishes
    - Chopped cilantro
    - Lime wedges

Instructions:

1. **Prepare the Steak:**
    - In a skillet, heat olive oil over high heat. Season the steak with taco seasoning, salt, and pepper. Sauté for 3-4 minutes until cooked to your liking.
2. **Make the Avocado Cream:**
    - In a blender or food processor, combine avocado, sour cream, lime juice, and salt. Blend until smooth.
3. **Warm the Tortillas:**
    - Warm the tortillas in a dry skillet over medium heat.
4. **Assemble the Tacos:**
    - Fill each tortilla with sizzling steak, drizzle with avocado cream, and top with sliced radishes and chopped cilantro. Serve with lime wedges.

Lentil and Sweet Potato Tacos

Ingredients:

- **For the Filling:**
    - 1 cup cooked lentils
    - 1 medium sweet potato, diced and roasted
    - 1 teaspoon cumin
    - 1 teaspoon smoked paprika
    - Salt and pepper to taste
    - 8 small corn or flour tortillas
- **Toppings:**
    - Shredded lettuce
    - Diced tomatoes
    - Avocado slices
    - Lime wedges

Instructions:

1. **Prepare the Filling:**
    - In a skillet, combine cooked lentils, roasted sweet potato, cumin, smoked paprika, salt, and pepper. Cook for 5 minutes until heated through.
2. **Warm the Tortillas:**
    - Warm the tortillas in a dry skillet over medium heat.
3. **Assemble the Tacos:**
    - Fill each tortilla with lentil and sweet potato mixture and top with shredded lettuce, diced tomatoes, and avocado slices. Serve with lime wedges.

Tacos de Carnitas with Cilantro and Onion

Ingredients:

- **For the Carnitas:**
    - 2 lbs pork shoulder, cooked and shredded
    - 1 tablespoon cumin
    - 1 tablespoon oregano
    - Salt and pepper to taste
    - 8 small corn or flour tortillas
- **Toppings:**
    - Chopped onions
    - Fresh cilantro
    - Lime wedges
    - Salsa of your choice

Instructions:

1. **Prepare the Carnitas:**
    - In a skillet, heat cooked pork with cumin, oregano, salt, and pepper until crispy on the edges.
2. **Warm the Tortillas:**
    - Warm the tortillas in a dry skillet over medium heat.
3. **Assemble the Tacos:**
    - Fill each tortilla with carnitas, top with chopped onions and fresh cilantro. Serve with lime wedges and salsa.

Roasted Vegetable Tacos with Feta

Ingredients:

- **For the Vegetables:**
    - 1 zucchini, diced
    - 1 bell pepper, diced
    - 1 red onion, sliced
    - 2 tablespoons olive oil
    - Salt and pepper to taste
    - 8 small corn or flour tortillas
- **Toppings:**
    - 1 cup crumbled feta cheese
    - Fresh basil or cilantro, for garnish
    - Balsamic glaze (optional)

Instructions:

1. **Roast the Vegetables:**
    - Preheat the oven to 425°F (220°C). Toss zucchini, bell pepper, and red onion with olive oil, salt, and pepper. Spread on a baking sheet and roast for 20-25 minutes until tender.
2. **Warm the Tortillas:**
    - Warm the tortillas in a dry skillet over medium heat.
3. **Assemble the Tacos:**
    - Fill each tortilla with roasted vegetables, sprinkle with crumbled feta, and garnish with fresh basil or cilantro. Drizzle with balsamic glaze if desired.

Hawaiian BBQ Chicken Tacos

Ingredients:

- **For the Chicken:**
    - 1 lb boneless, skinless chicken thighs
    - 1 cup BBQ sauce (preferably Hawaiian style)
    - 1 tablespoon olive oil
    - Salt and pepper to taste
    - 8 small corn or flour tortillas
- **For the Toppings:**
    - 1 cup pineapple, diced
    - 1/2 red onion, thinly sliced
    - 1 cup shredded cabbage
    - Fresh cilantro, for garnish
    - Lime wedges

Instructions:

1. **Prepare the Chicken:**
    - In a skillet, heat olive oil over medium heat. Season chicken with salt and pepper and cook for 5-7 minutes per side until cooked through. Shred the chicken and mix with BBQ sauce.
2. **Warm the Tortillas:**
    - Warm the tortillas in a dry skillet over medium heat.
3. **Assemble the Tacos:**
    - Fill each tortilla with BBQ chicken, top with diced pineapple, sliced red onion, and shredded cabbage. Garnish with fresh cilantro and serve with lime wedges.

These recipes offer a great variety of flavors and ingredients, perfect for any taco night! Enjoy!

Chipotle Black Bean Tacos with Corn Salsa

Ingredients:

- **For the Tacos:**
    - 1 can (15 oz) black beans, rinsed and drained
    - 1 tablespoon chipotle in adobo sauce, chopped
    - 1 teaspoon cumin
    - Salt and pepper to taste
    - 8 small corn or flour tortillas
- **For the Corn Salsa:**
    - 1 cup corn (fresh, frozen, or canned)
    - 1/2 red onion, diced
    - 1 jalapeño, minced (optional)
    - Juice of 1 lime
    - 1/4 cup fresh cilantro, chopped
    - Salt to taste

Instructions:

1. **Prepare the Black Beans:**
    - In a skillet, combine black beans, chipotle, cumin, salt, and pepper. Heat over medium heat until warmed through.
2. **Make the Corn Salsa:**
    - In a bowl, mix corn, red onion, jalapeño, lime juice, cilantro, and salt. Stir to combine.
3. **Warm the Tortillas:**
    - Warm the tortillas in a dry skillet over medium heat.
4. **Assemble the Tacos:**
    - Fill each tortilla with black beans and top with corn salsa. Serve immediately.

Mahi Mahi Tacos with Cilantro Lime Sauce

Ingredients:

- **For the Fish:**
    - 1 lb mahi mahi fillets
    - 2 tablespoons olive oil
    - 1 teaspoon cumin
    - Salt and pepper to taste
    - 8 small corn or flour tortillas
- **For the Cilantro Lime Sauce:**
    - 1/2 cup Greek yogurt or sour cream
    - 1/4 cup fresh cilantro, chopped
    - Juice of 1 lime
    - 1 clove garlic, minced
    - Salt to taste
- **Toppings:**
    - Shredded cabbage
    - Diced tomatoes
    - Lime wedges

Instructions:

1. **Prepare the Fish:**
    - Preheat the grill or skillet over medium-high heat. Season mahi mahi with olive oil, cumin, salt, and pepper. Cook for 4-5 minutes per side until cooked through. Flake the fish.
2. **Make the Sauce:**
    - In a bowl, mix Greek yogurt, cilantro, lime juice, garlic, and salt until combined.
3. **Warm the Tortillas:**
    - Warm the tortillas in a dry skillet over medium heat.
4. **Assemble the Tacos:**
    - Fill each tortilla with mahi mahi, drizzle with cilantro lime sauce, and top with shredded cabbage and diced tomatoes. Serve with lime wedges.

Turkey and Sweet Potato Tacos

Ingredients:

- **For the Filling:**
    - 1 lb ground turkey
    - 1 medium sweet potato, peeled and diced
    - 1 teaspoon cumin
    - 1 teaspoon paprika
    - Salt and pepper to taste
    - 8 small corn or flour tortillas
- **Toppings:**
    - Sliced avocado
    - Chopped cilantro
    - Lime wedges

Instructions:

1. **Prepare the Filling:**
    - In a skillet, cook diced sweet potato in a bit of water until tender. Drain and set aside. In the same skillet, cook ground turkey with cumin, paprika, salt, and pepper until browned. Add sweet potatoes and mix.
2. **Warm the Tortillas:**
    - Warm the tortillas in a dry skillet over medium heat.
3. **Assemble the Tacos:**
    - Fill each tortilla with the turkey and sweet potato mixture and top with sliced avocado and chopped cilantro. Serve with lime wedges.

Tacos de Barbacoa with Red Chili Sauce

Ingredients:

- **For the Barbacoa:**
    - 2 lbs beef chuck roast
    - 1 onion, chopped
    - 3 cloves garlic, minced
    - 1 tablespoon cumin
    - 1 tablespoon oregano
    - 1 cup beef broth
    - Salt and pepper to taste
    - 8 small corn or flour tortillas
- **For the Red Chili Sauce:**
    - 3 dried red chilies, seeds removed
    - 1 cup hot water
    - 1 clove garlic
    - Salt to taste

Instructions:

1. **Prepare the Barbacoa:**
    - In a slow cooker, combine beef, onion, garlic, cumin, oregano, beef broth, salt, and pepper. Cook on low for 8 hours or until tender. Shred the beef.
2. **Make the Red Chili Sauce:**
    - In a blender, combine soaked chilies, hot water, garlic, and salt. Blend until smooth.
3. **Warm the Tortillas:**
    - Warm the tortillas in a dry skillet over medium heat.
4. **Assemble the Tacos:**
    - Fill each tortilla with barbacoa and drizzle with red chili sauce.

Mexican Street Corn Tacos

Ingredients:

- **For the Corn:**
    - 2 cups corn (fresh or frozen)
    - 2 tablespoons mayonnaise
    - 1/4 cup crumbled cotija cheese
    - 1 tablespoon lime juice
    - 1 teaspoon chili powder
    - Salt to taste
    - 8 small corn or flour tortillas

Instructions:

1. **Prepare the Corn:**
    - In a skillet, cook corn until slightly charred. Remove from heat and mix with mayonnaise, cotija cheese, lime juice, chili powder, and salt.
2. **Warm the Tortillas:**
    - Warm the tortillas in a dry skillet over medium heat.
3. **Assemble the Tacos:**
    - Fill each tortilla with the corn mixture and serve immediately.

Vegetable Fajita Tacos

Ingredients:

- **For the Fajitas:**
    - 1 bell pepper, sliced
    - 1 zucchini, sliced
    - 1 onion, sliced
    - 2 tablespoons olive oil
    - 1 teaspoon cumin
    - Salt and pepper to taste
    - 8 small corn or flour tortillas
- **Toppings:**
    - Avocado slices
    - Fresh cilantro
    - Lime wedges

Instructions:

1. **Prepare the Fajitas:**
    - In a skillet, heat olive oil over medium heat. Add bell pepper, zucchini, and onion. Season with cumin, salt, and pepper. Sauté until tender.
2. **Warm the Tortillas:**
    - Warm the tortillas in a dry skillet over medium heat.
3. **Assemble the Tacos:**
    - Fill each tortilla with sautéed vegetables and top with avocado slices and fresh cilantro. Serve with lime wedges.

Pork Belly Tacos with Jalapeño Slaw

Ingredients:

- **For the Pork Belly:**
    - 1 lb pork belly, diced
    - 2 tablespoons olive oil
    - Salt and pepper to taste
    - 8 small corn or flour tortillas
- **For the Jalapeño Slaw:**
    - 2 cups shredded cabbage
    - 1 jalapeño, thinly sliced
    - 1/4 cup mayonnaise
    - Juice of 1 lime
    - Salt to taste

Instructions:

1. **Prepare the Pork Belly:**
    - In a skillet, heat olive oil over medium-high heat. Add pork belly and cook until crispy. Season with salt and pepper.
2. **Make the Jalapeño Slaw:**
    - In a bowl, combine shredded cabbage, jalapeño, mayonnaise, lime juice, and salt. Mix well.
3. **Warm the Tortillas:**
    - Warm the tortillas in a dry skillet over medium heat.
4. **Assemble the Tacos:**
    - Fill each tortilla with crispy pork belly and top with jalapeño slaw. Serve immediately.

These recipes offer a delightful variety of flavors and ingredients for your taco night! Enjoy!

Crispy Chickpea Tacos

Ingredients:

- **For the Tacos:**
    - 1 can (15 oz) chickpeas, rinsed and drained
    - 2 tablespoons olive oil
    - 1 teaspoon smoked paprika
    - 1 teaspoon cumin
    - Salt and pepper to taste
    - 8 small corn or flour tortillas
- **For the Toppings:**
    - Shredded cabbage
    - Diced tomatoes
    - Avocado slices
    - Fresh cilantro
    - Lime wedges

Instructions:

1. **Prepare the Chickpeas:**
    - Preheat the oven to 400°F (200°C). In a bowl, toss chickpeas with olive oil, smoked paprika, cumin, salt, and pepper. Spread on a baking sheet and roast for 20-25 minutes until crispy.
2. **Warm the Tortillas:**
    - Warm the tortillas in a dry skillet over medium heat.
3. **Assemble the Tacos:**
    - Fill each tortilla with crispy chickpeas and top with shredded cabbage, diced tomatoes, avocado slices, and fresh cilantro. Serve with lime wedges.

Sriracha Shrimp Tacos with Avocado Salsa

Ingredients:

- **For the Shrimp:**
    - 1 lb shrimp, peeled and deveined
    - 2 tablespoons olive oil
    - 1 tablespoon sriracha sauce
    - Salt and pepper to taste
    - 8 small corn or flour tortillas
- **For the Avocado Salsa:**
    - 1 avocado, diced
    - 1/2 red onion, diced
    - 1 tomato, diced
    - Juice of 1 lime
    - Salt to taste

Instructions:

1. **Prepare the Shrimp:**
    - In a skillet, heat olive oil over medium heat. Toss shrimp with sriracha, salt, and pepper. Cook for 3-4 minutes until shrimp are pink and cooked through.
2. **Make the Avocado Salsa:**
    - In a bowl, combine avocado, red onion, tomato, lime juice, and salt. Mix gently.
3. **Warm the Tortillas:**
    - Warm the tortillas in a dry skillet over medium heat.
4. **Assemble the Tacos:**
    - Fill each tortilla with sriracha shrimp and top with avocado salsa.

Taco Salad Bowls

Ingredients:

- **For the Salad:**
    - 1 lb ground beef or turkey
    - 1 packet taco seasoning
    - 4 cups romaine lettuce, chopped
    - 1 can (15 oz) black beans, rinsed and drained
    - 1 cup corn (fresh, frozen, or canned)
    - 1 cup diced tomatoes
    - 1 cup shredded cheese (cheddar or Mexican blend)
    - 1/2 cup salsa
    - 1/4 cup sour cream
    - Tortilla chips for garnish

Instructions:

1. **Cook the Meat:**
    - In a skillet, cook ground beef or turkey over medium heat until browned. Drain excess fat, add taco seasoning, and follow package instructions.
2. **Assemble the Salad Bowls:**
    - In bowls, layer romaine lettuce, black beans, corn, diced tomatoes, cooked meat, shredded cheese, salsa, and sour cream. Top with tortilla chips.

Mini Taco Cups with Taco Meat

Ingredients:

- **For the Taco Meat:**
    - 1 lb ground beef or turkey
    - 1 packet taco seasoning
    - 1/2 cup water
    - 1 package wonton wrappers (14 oz)
- **For the Toppings:**
    - Shredded cheese
    - Diced tomatoes
    - Shredded lettuce
    - Sour cream
    - Salsa

Instructions:

1. **Prepare the Taco Meat:**
    - In a skillet, cook ground beef or turkey over medium heat until browned. Drain excess fat, add taco seasoning and water, and simmer until thickened.
2. **Make the Taco Cups:**
    - Preheat the oven to 375°F (190°C). Grease a muffin tin. Press wonton wrappers into muffin cups, and bake for 5-7 minutes until crispy.
3. **Assemble the Taco Cups:**
    - Fill each wonton cup with taco meat and top with shredded cheese, diced tomatoes, shredded lettuce, sour cream, and salsa. Serve warm.

Enjoy these tasty taco recipes that are sure to please a crowd!

www.ingramcontent.com/pod-product-compliance
Lightning Source LLC
LaVergne TN
LVHW081319060526
838201LV00055B/2374